THE INITIATION
CATHY PETOCZ

CURRENCY PRESS
The performing arts publisher

CURRENT THEATRE SERIES

First published in 2022
by Currency Press Pty Ltd,
PO Box 2287, Strawberry Hills, NSW, 2012, Australia
enquiries@currency.com.au
www.currency.com.au
in association with Canberra Youth Theatre.

Copyright: *The Initiation* © Cathy Petőcz, 2022.

COPYING FOR EDUCATIONAL PURPOSES
The Australian *Copyright Act 1968* [Act] allows a maximum of one chapter or 10% of this book, whichever is the greater, to be copied by any educational institution for its educational purposes provided that that educational institution [or the body that administers it] has given a remuneration notice to Copyright Agency [CA] under the Act.

For details of the CA licence for educational institutions contact CA, 11/66 Goulburn Street, Sydney, NSW, 2000; tel: within Australia 1800 066 844 toll free; outside Australia 61 2 9394 7600; fax: 61 2 9394 7601; email: info@copyright.com.au

COPYING FOR OTHER PURPOSES
Except as permitted under the Act, for example a fair dealing for the purposes of study, research, criticism or review, no part of this book may be reproduced, stored in a retrieval system, or transmitted in any form or by any means without prior written permission. All enquiries should be made to the publisher at the address above.

Any performance or public reading of *The Initiation* is forbidden unless a licence has been received from the author or the author's agent. The purchase of this book in no way gives the purchaser the right to perform the play in public, whether by means of a staged production or a reading. All applications for public performance should be addressed to the author c/- Currency Press

Typeset by Brighton Gray for Currency Press.
Cover shows, L-R: Thomas Bigsby-Chamberlin, Latsamy Carruthers, Disa Swifte, Danni Allen, Tara Saxena and Persephone Bates d'Arbela.
Cover image by Adam McGrath/Hcreations.

Currency Press acknowledges the Traditional Owners of the Country on which we live and work. We pay our respects to all Aboriginal and Torres Strait Islander Elders, past and present.

 A catalogue record for this book is available from the National Library of Australia

Contents

THE INITIATION　　　　　　　　　　　　　　　1

Theatre Program at the end of the playtext

The Initiation was first produced by Canberra Youth Theatre at The Courtyard Studio, Canberra Theatre Centre, on 15 June 2022, with the following cast:

REBECCA / SEB	Sylvie Burke
ERIS	Latsamy Carruthers
FEY	Zoe Harris
AMELIA	Juniper Potter
CHRIS	Tara Saxena
LIAM	Harry Ziarno

Director, Cathy Petocz
Set and Costume Designer, Nyx Mathews
Lighting Designer, Gillian Schwab
Sound Designer, Patrick Haesler
Assistant Director, Caitlin Baker
Stage Manager, Rhiley Winnett
Dramaturgy and Cultural Support, Ethan Bell

This play was developed with Canberra Youth Theatre young artists: Danni Allen, Imogen Atkinson, Thomas Bigsby-Chamberlin, Sylvie Burke, Latsamy Carruthers, Stephanie Hudson, Elian Louchart-Fletcher, Bridie Mackay, Juniper Potter, Tara Saxena, Zoe Smith and Christopher Want.

CHARACTERS

FEY, 15. A quick-thinking overachiever who is afraid she might not be able to believe in God anymore.

REBECCA, 15. The girl who used to be impatient to grow up is now feeling weird about leaving childhood behind.

LIAM, 14. a quiet, nerdy boy who can't figure out how he will approach becoming a man in the age of toxic masculinity.

CHRIS, 15. A rational, politically progressive teenage private eye who feels inexplicably terrified by and drawn to another girl in the group.

AMELIA, 14. The self-made outsider, she is having huge trouble dealing with anything at all and secretly hurting herself is the only way to feel okay.

ERIS (STRIFE), 15. A haughty mean girl who is actually a thousands-year-old supernatural being who needs to be reunited with her sword (The Knife) in order to return to her magical realm.

SEB, early 20s. Fey's older brother. He is a voiceover only (possibly the voice of the actor playing Rebecca except pitched down).

THROUGH FEY, a voice speaking through Fey.

SETTINGS

The play takes place on Ngunnawal / Ngambri Country.

First and last, the fairly posh suburb of Turner: David Street in particular and the threshold of Barry Drive.

But mostly, the wilds of Black Mountain.

The play takes place over one night, from twilight to dawn, from one liminality to another.

Once in the bush of Black Mountain, time moves around in an unreliable way, it splits into two (or more) threads which all happen at the same time.

RULES OF THE WORLD

The Knife is a shapeshifting being which transforms according to the desires and needs of the person who beholds and holds it. Others see it in the form the bearer co-creates, for example: Liam spies and picks up a machete and the others see The Knife as a machete at that time. Eris knows The Knife is who it is.

Actors keep the bloodstains from previous scenes, even if that reality is not true in the scene being played.

This play text went to press before the end of rehearsals and may differ from the play as performed.

SCENE 0

As the audience enters, ERIS *is eating a bright red toffee apple on a stick. The apple is the Earth to* ERIS.

There is a terrible sound brewing, but it is growing very gradually. There is also the sound of her eating, which is unnoticeable at first but becomes full-strength ASMR, then beyond.

This is ERIS' *last meal before she leaves Earth. She is thinking about how she used to love it here but now she hates it, she is sick of humanity. The sound is her resolve to leave, her anger at being stuck here for so long. She is gathering herself up, getting ready.*

SCENE 1

When the audience is in, the house lights down, the sound and the feeling grows until she finishes the toffee apple. The sound is almost unbearable.

ERIS *quells the unbearable sound somewhat, still present as she speaks ... She uses the stick to carve out* CHRIS*'s name in the ground. A love spell.*

During her speech, the teens are introduced in a strobe-lit, flickering sequence of horror-type jump-cut images, as described below the speech. This should build a sense of threat.

ERIS: Apple on a stick
   It makes me sick
   It makes my heart beat two-forty-six
   Not because you're dirty
   Not because you're clean
   Not because you kissed the boy behind the magazine
   Girls, boys, having fun
   Here comes the lady with the big fat bum
   She can wiggle, she can waggle
   She can even do the splits
   But I bet you

I bet you
She can't do this
Close your eyes and count to ten
If you muck it up, you're not my friend
One, two, three, four, five, six, seven, eight, nine, ten—

> CHRIS *twirls a pen without noticing. She is thinking about* ERIS.
>
> REBECCA *cuts a pair of denim shorts shorter.*
>
> FEY *exercises furiously with headphones on.*
>
> LIAM *plays a violent video game.*
>
> AMELIA *reads a book to distract herself but it's not working.*
>
> FEY *does the plank-based mountain-climbing exercise and stops, pulling off her headphones—she thought she heard something.*
>
> LIAM *plays the game and makes a great kill and smiles.*
>
> CHRIS *sees something by torchlight that disgusts and scares her.*
>
> AMELIA *drops the heavy book and rolls up her sleeve.*
>
> REBECCA *puts lipstick on.*
>
> *Then, all at the same time ...*
>
> AMELIA *watches the cut on her arm bleed, then stops it by pressing it to her mouth.*
>
> CHRIS *writes about* ERIS.
>
> REBECCA *wipes the lipstick off.*
>
> LIAM *gets killed and flinches.*
>
> FEY *has a panic attack with her phone pressed to her ear waiting for* REBECCA *to pick up.*
>
> *As* ERIS *counts, they all become aware of a weird taste and discover their mouths are filled with blood. It oozes out, they cough it up, spit it out, and they are terrified.*

You didn't muck it up so you're my best—

> *The Knife is revealed in a flash of light. We don't know who is holding it.*

I'm gonna get you.

ERIS *rapidly plunges the toffee apple stick into the ground and jumps up and dashes off stage.*

ERIS *has summoned The Knife.*

SCENE 2

CHRIS *enters, checks no-one is watching, and creeps up to the site of the spell. She pulls out a plastic baggie and tweezers, and bags up the stick. Then she sees her name scratched into the ground and is suitably freaked out.*

The sound of a horror movie scream as a window opens. CHRIS *is doubly freaked.*

FEY *and* REBECCA *climb out of a window.* CHRIS *is relieved.*

REBECCA *and* FEY *try not to make too much sound but laugh and shush each other as they clumsily escape. When they are both out, they are pleased with themselves: freedom!*

CHRIS: Where are you two going?

    FEY *and* REBECCA *scream.*

REBECCA: Oh my god, Chris! / What are you doing here?
FEY: Shhhhh!
CHRIS: Nothing!
FEY: [*noticing her brother through the window*] Oh brother: Seb's sneaking beers again. Dad's gonna kill you!
REBECCA: Let's get out of here. Come with?
CHRIS: Where are you going?
FEY: Out. We don't know. Anywhere!
REBECCA: Gotta get away from Seb—
FEY: My big brother. He's watching this lame-ass horror movie we're not allowed to watch so we're fucking getting outta here.
CHRIS: Fey Chrysler! School Captain, Dux-of-the-School, ballet dancer, elite debater, advanced-maths-extended-Fey … Did you just say the f-word?
FEY: What the fucking fuck are you fucking talking about?
CHRIS: Okayyyyy … Chill Miss Rebel.

    LIAM *walks past in the distance.*

REBECCA: Who's that?
CHRIS: It's Liam. He goes to my school, the grade below us. I see him in the library a lot.
REBECCA: He looks like a serial killer. Hey! What's his name again—Liam? Liam! Hey Liam! Li-am! Come over here!
FEY: [*to* REBECCA] What are you doing??

> LIAM *approaches uncertainly.*

REBECCA: Let's have a bit of fun. Hey Liam. Whatcha up to?
LIAM: Just heading home. [*To* CHRIS] Hey.
CHRIS: Hey.
REBECCA: Where from?
LIAM: Uhhhh … Just the library. Just studying.
CHRIS: I told you! He basically lives in the library. You probably only left because it closed.
LIAM: Yeah well …
REBECCA: What were you studying? Lesbian porn?
FEY: [*laughing*] Oh my god, Becca!
LIAM: Ah, no.
REBECCA: You're not interested in the female anatomy?
LIAM: No, it's—
REBECCA: He's gay.
CHRIS: Becca, leave him alone!
LIAM: I'm not gay.
FEY: Oh he's not *gay* …
CHRIS: Cool. Cos we don't shame people about their sexuality—
FEY: … he's an axe murderer! He was looking up how to sharpen his axe!
REBECCA: He was looking up how to seduce his victims.
FEY: And chop up the bodies!
REBECCA: Now I get it, and we're totally cool with your sexuality, you like DEAD BODIES. / Blue lips, stiff limbs, staring eyes, stone cold—
FEY: Ew! Necrophilia!
LIAM: [*bursting out*] I was looking up how to be a man!

> *Everyone is so stunned, no-one even laughs.*
>
> LIAM *starts to charge away but* REBECCA *cuts him off.*

REBECCA: How to be a man?
CHRIS: Screw you Becca. But seriously Liam, at the library?
LIAM: Our computer is in the living room and I'm not looking it up there in the middle of our house. And I don't have a phone. My mum's really strict. So I just … I just waited until nearly everyone had left the library and I just quickly Googled, just looked at the WikiHow for a second …
REBECCA: What did it say?
FEY: Yeah, oh my god, what did it say?
CHRIS: Shut up, guys.
LIAM: Why don't you just look it up yourselves?

> AMELIA *floats out of her house in her own world.*
>
> *They all watch her.*
>
> *She freezes when she sees them.*

AMELIA: What are you looking at?
FEY: We're looking up how to be a man!!
LIAM: Can you just drop it?
CHRIS: They're torturing him.
AMELIA: Do it.

> *She snatches the phone from* FEY.

What's better, look up how to be a woman. It's fucking gnarly.
FEY: Um! That's my phone! Who are you? Who is she?
CHRIS: Amelia.
LIAM: We all go to school together.
CHRIS: [*about* FEY *and* REBECCA] We do debating together.
FEY: We go to Edgecliff Girls.
AMELIA: [*looking at* REBECCA] And we used to be best friends.
REBECCA: Hi Amelia. Awkward much?
FEY: Ohhhhh, this is the—
AMELIA: The what?
FEY: Oh sorry, nothing. I just meant—
AMELIA: What?
REBECCA: Nothing.
AMELIA: You saying shit about me, Rebecca?
FEY: No, she just—

REBECCA: Amelia … We used to be friends, I moved schools, we lost touch. No biggie.
AMELIA: [*clutching The Knife in her pocket*] WHAT ARE YOU FUCKING SAYING ABOUT ME?
CHRIS: I've literally never heard either of you talk about the other.
REBECCA: Millie, chill.
AMELIA: DON'T FUCKING TELL ME TO CHILL.
CHRIS: Yeah that's the worst! Like when has the command CALM DOWN ever worked?
LIAM: Makes my mum go crazy.
CHRIS: Sooooooo! How do I become a woman? It's my lifelong dream so …
AMELIA: What?
CHRIS: Lay the Wiki on me!
AMELIA: Well. First of all, it's actually how to be a Lady. Nothing on 'woman' at all. There are only three parts: Behaving Like a Lady, Dressing Like a Lady, and Proper Table Etiquette.
FEY: That's ridiculous.
AMELIA: Like I said.
REBECCA: What does it say about behaving like a lady?
AMELIA: Make thoughtful introductions. Have good posture. Don't overeat or drink excessively. Know when to say no.
CHRIS: I say No to WikiHow and say Yes to doing whatever the hell I want.
FEY: Yeah, gross!
AMELIA: And check out how different How to Be a Man is: Know yourself. Be knowledgable about something.
LIAM: It's not that helpful. Be a *good* man, know the man-code.
REBECCA: What the fuck is the man-code?
LIAM: No idea.
AMELIA: [*laughing hysterically*] Clean yourself!! It actually says that. Oh my god, I'm instantly gay.
FEY: That's so real!
CHRIS: Uh, it doesn't work like that.
AMELIA: Don't tell me how my sexuality works!
FEY: Yeah, Chris—we don't shame each other about our sexuality.
LIAM: Not this again.

CHRIS: But you don't just instantly become gay. Sexuality doesn't work that way.

    ERIS *appears.*

ERIS: How does it work?

    Beat.

CHRIS: You just know. I mean, don't you? Like, it feels right. Being straight. Or whatever. Feels … Bleh! … Sorry … Hello. I'm Chris. I've seen you around … the place. You're …

ERIS: Eris.

    Pause.

AMELIA: Thoughtful introduction, Chris, one hundred percent thoughtful introduction. You're definitely on your way to being a capital-L Lady.

CHRIS: Bugger off.

REBECCA: I've seen you around too.

FEY: Do you live around here?

    ERIS *waves her hand towards nothing dismissively. Then she looks at* LIAM.

ERIS: You want to be a man?

REBECCA: Were you like eavesdropping on us?

ERIS: You want to be a man? Know what kind of man to be? It's an important question.

FEY: Especially in the age of toxic masculinity.

ERIS: Tell us.

LIAM: Well, yeah.

ERIS: I know a ritual for manhood. It requires entrance into a forest.

AMELIA: Black Mountain is like five minutes that way.

ERIS: It requires desire. You want to be a man, Liam?

LIAM: I guess so. I mean, obviously.

ERIS: The ritual requires five innocents.

FEY: This is creepy.

ERIS: We go with you.

REBECCA: What? Climb Black Mountain and have our way with him? Make him a man?

ERIS: We don't make him a man, he makes himself. There's a place in the bush balanced between stone, sky, water. Past stars sending ancient light. You'll find what you need for the initiation and you will come out changed.

AMELIA: [*feeling a jolt of courage from The Knife*] Let's do it. Too scared, Rebecca?

REBECCA: No, I just don't want to do some weird sex ritual with some dude who looks up how to be a man on WikiHow!

LIAM: I told you, I just—

ERIS: This isn't about sex.

REBECCA: Yeah, the more you say it, the more I'm convinced.

ERIS: Do you want it to be about sex?

REBECCA: No.

ERIS: So it's not.

CHRIS: Are you up for it, Liam?

LIAM: Uh, what?

CHRIS: Whatever this is.

REBECCA: Going up Black Mountain tonight and *not* doing a weird sex ritual.

LIAM: I guess so.

REBECCA: He wants to do the sex ritual.

AMELIA: Well, someone definitely wants to!

ERIS: [*to* CHRIS] And you?

CHRIS: I'm—I'm game. Fey?

FEY: I don't know. We probably have to get back.

REBECCA: Your parents are away.

FEY: Yeah but …

REBECCA: And Seb won't tell.

FEY: He probably hasn't even noticed we're gone.

REBECCA: We'll be back before morning.

FEY: Don't we have debating tomorrow morning?

CHRIS: Cancelled.

REBECCA: So, we're doing it.

FEY: Yeah, I guess for a bit.

AMELIA: We're going! [*Singing*] Gonna climb a spooky mountain. Gonna do a creepy ritual!!

ERIS: We go.

SCENE 3

They walk towards Barry Drive, a multi-lane road, the threshold they must cross.

CHRIS *and* ERIS *lead the way with the other teens awkwardly chatting behind them.*

CHRIS: So you're a witch?
ERIS: Sort of, so what?
CHRIS: I don't believe in magic.
ERIS: You will.
CHRIS: Hahaha, yeah nah. I'm more of a science-meets-reality girl.
ERIS: Want to bet on it?
CHRIS: One hundred percent. What's the bet?
ERIS: Before daybreak you will pull out your own heart and let me eat from it.
CHRIS: Pull out my own heart.
ERIS: And let me eat it.
CHRIS: Literally or figuratively I really don't think that will happen. What do I get if I win? If I don't somehow happen to pull out my own heart and offer it to you for a midnight snack.
ERIS: Whatever you want. And what do I get?
CHRIS: If you've already eaten from my beating heart? Isn't that enough?
ERIS: I'll get to go home.

    They've reached the edge of Barry Drive.

Time to cross the threshold. We don't come back until we finish the initiation.
LIAM: I don't have to kill an animal, do I?
ERIS: Maybe.
LIAM: Maybe we should just—
AMELIA: Just what?
LIAM: I probably should be going.
REBECCA: [*covered by an obvious cough*] Pussy.
FEY: I don't know if I want to go either.

REBECCA: What?? Whyyyyyyyyyyy??
FEY: Wellllllll … Black Mountain is a sacred site. I read it on a sign in Haig Park. So maybe we shouldn't go there?
LIAM: You're probably right.
CHRIS: We won't leave the path!
AMELIA: Telstra Tower is like already ruining everything anyway! But true.
LIAM: My Year Five teacher said 'Respect Country and Country will respect you.'

The teens turn to go.

ERIS: Country … wants something from me … [*To* FEY] How do you feel?
FEY: Afraid … [*looking at* REBECCA] but excited.
ERIS: Go.

Without thinking, FEY *runs across the road screaming.*

ERIS *grabs Chris' hand.*

Now us.

They run.

REBECCA: Nice boots.
AMELIA: Fuck off.
REBECCA: No really! You look good. I mean, different, but good. Tough.
AMELIA: Thanks?
REBECCA: Oh my god, forget it.
AMELIA: I like this private school slut thing you've got going on.
REBECCA: Last one there's a fucking bitch who can't get over the past!

They tear across the road.

LIAM *is left, having serious second thoughts. He's just about to turn around and go home.*

ERIS: Make your choice, Liam! Cross the threshold!
CHRIS: Come on, Liam!
AMELIA: Hurry up!
REBECCA: Don't be a pussy!
FEY: Puuuussyyyyyy!!
CHRIS: Guys, don't. Just come on Liam!
FEY: We'll tell everyone you're a wimp!!
AMELIA: Go home if you can't deal!

REBECCA: Do you want to be a virgin forever??
CHRIS: Oh my god shut up!
AMELIA: Be a man, Liam!
FEY: [*starting a chant*] Be a man! Be a man!

> *Everyone laughs and chants—though not* ERIS *who watches the cruelty with interest—and* LIAM *who freaks out and tries really hard not to show it.*

REBECCA: [*changing the chant*] Puuuuuussyyyyyyy! Puuuuuussyyyyyyy!

> LIAM *can't bear it anymore and just does it, he runs across the road.*
>
> *The girls cheer and run off.*
>
> LIAM *starts to have a panic attack. He tries to calm himself down but it's not helping.*
>
> *He bends over to get control of his breathing and catches sight of something metal glinting on the ground.*
>
> *It is The Knife in the form of a machete. He picks it up and as soon as he touches it, it calms him. He straightens up and admires it in the streetlight, giving it a couple of slashes through the air. It feels good.*

AMELIA: [*from offstage*] Come on, Pussyyyyy!

> *He looks after the girls, admires The Knife and grips it more firmly, and runs after them.*
>
> *The image should appear ominous, like perhaps he might murder them.*

SCENE 4

They all make their way through the bush with a couple of torches from their phones. Time has jumped forward and LIAM *does not have The Knife.*

FEY: Never have I ever talked back to a teacher.
AMELIA: I have.
REBECCA: Yeah, me.
CHRIS: And me.

LIAM: Not me.
FEY: Okay … Go Becca.
REBECCA: Never have I ever … kissed a boy … / ro-man-tic-ly.
FEY: Yes you have! Oh.
LIAM: Not me.
FEY: What kiss is not romantic?
AMELIA: Like fully mashing lips is not romantic.
LIAM: Yeah, eating someone's face off is hardly romantic. I know that much.
REBECCA: No, I mean, like kissing when you feel romantic about it.
CHRIS: You've kissed someone. How did you feel about it?
REBECCA: Morbid curiosity!
FEY: True dat.
REBECCA: So, anyone?

>   *Pause.*

Wow. Romance is dead.
FEY: You said kissed a boy romantically.
CHRIS: Such a homophobe Becca!
REBECCA: Yeah whoops! Never have I ever kissed someone romantically.

>   *Pause.*

Damn. Even gay romance is dead.
FEY: We're only fourteen! Give us time!
ERIS: I have.
AMELIA: Was it good?
ERIS: What do you think?
REBECCA: Your go.
ERIS: Never have … I ever … received a gift.
FEY: What?? That's crazy!
AMELIA: [*to* CHRIS] What the fuuuuck??
CHRIS: [*low voice*] Homeschooler.
ERIS: Have you all?
ALL: Yeah. [*etc.*]
ERIS: Well then.
CHRIS: My go. Never have I ever … this is hard.
REBECCA: Why? Because you've done so much!
CHRIS: Shut up. Never have I ever … heard voices.

LIAM: Like in your mind?
CHRIS: Like you hear voices … You know, and no-one's there.
AMELIA: Like ghosts or like schizophrenia?
CHRIS: I don't know! I'm trying to be spooky. We're in a forest, it's night. Someone's got to amp up the horror a bit.
LIAM: Yeah, nah.
ERIS: Not me.
REBECCA: Me either.
AMELIA: Nope.
CHRIS: Fey?
FEY: Well …
CHRIS: STORY TIME.
FEY: When I am very quiet and I listen, not too carefully but like I'm so relaxed I let go of everything, even listening, sometimes … I hear a voice.

During the monologue the others melt away into darkness.

I see a therapist. She asks me in our first session, Do you hear voices? And I am offended. Like, I know she's asking because it's on the checklist but I feel like the checklist is issuing a form of normal I'm not okay with.

Like, yes, I sometimes hear a voice and I wish I heard it more. Like, my life would be better if I could hear it more clearly. I wouldn't be here with YOU, a therapist asking me if I *hear voices*.

What does she mean anyway? Ghosts whispering? Multiple personalities? A little angel and devil duking it out on my shoulders? But that's like a metaphor for the conscience. So is she asking whether I have a mechanism for accessing my ethical feelings? She's asking if I have a sense of morality? And, how do we even know what is right and wrong if we don't listen to our inner voice?

This is just how fast my brain goes. This is why I go to therapy. But it's also why I get the best grades, and everyone thinks I'm smart—I'm not, my brain just goes fast and I need to keep it busy or it will go fast with other things like IS THIS THERAPIST ASKING IF I AM A MORAL PERSON? Everyone is like, HOW DID YOU GET FROM THERE TO THERE?? And I'm just trying to slow down enough to listen to the conversation.

Weird flex, I know. My parents love me being smart, obviously, and they hate that I'm anxious, also obviously. But it's the same thing—this whirlwind of my own thoughts—so why is one aspect okay and the other feared so much?

Why is pain so scary for everyone? Why do people panic when you cry in front of them? Why is everyone freaked out about death? It's all we have in common, really. We are all going to die. WE ARE ALL GONNA DIE.

And then I'm suffocating. In myself. In the currents of my own voice in my head, swirling faster and faster. And I want so badly to hear the other voice. Soft. Still. Certain.

Do you hear voices? My therapist holds her pen above the unchecked box.

What about God? I say.

Well, not in that way.

What way is that? I think.

But I say, No. I don't hear voices.

But I do sometimes hear a voice. And I wish I could hear it more. I feel like it's leaving me and that makes me feel very afraid.

REBECCA: Fey? Fey, are you okay?

Everyone else is back.

FEY: What?

CHRIS: You were just standing there babbling. Like, we couldn't understand you.

REBECCA: Are you okay? She might be having a stroke.

FEY: What? I'm fine.

AMELIA: Why does she have a knife?

FEY realises she is holding a meat cleaver. It is The Knife.

SCENE 5

Time jumps back. Everyone hangs around waiting for LIAM *to catch up from Barry Drive.* FEY *and The Knife hasn't happened yet.*

AMELIA: [*calling back to* LIAM] Come on, Pussyyyyy!

FEY: It was like an eighties slasher, you know, fluffy hairdos and full nude shots.

REBECCA: Yeah, the tagline is like: [*horror voice*] 'They pledge themselves to die young.'
FEY *and* BECCA: [*American sorority girl voices*] 'Here's to being young, staying young, and dying young!'
FEY: It's so bananas though, like a whole sorority being murdered in a mall with a garden fork or something.
CHRIS: If you weren't allowed to watch it, how do you know so much about it?
FEY: We watched the trailer.
REBECCA: There's this freaky shot of the murderer lifting up a machete, like just an arm and a giant knife lit up right before it—

> *There is a flash of light illuminating a shadow holding up a machete in the way* REBECCA *is describing.*
>
> REBECCA *screams.*
>
> LIAM *catches up to them and lifts The Knife to show them what he found. He doesn't realise the scream is about him and is startled.*

Oh my god, he's going to kill us!
LIAM: [*afraid*] Who?
AMELIA: You.
LIAM: No I'm not. I found this in the bushes. Cool, hey?
REBECCA: Yeah, you kinda scared us to death!
LIAM: Sorry.
ERIS: [*talking to The Knife but no-one realises*] Ah! You're with us finally.
CHRIS: Chill guys. It's not a movie. Murders don't really happen in forests on spooky nights.
AMELIA: Uh, they absolutely do! The Slender Man murder? Literally two twelve-year-olds stabbed their friend nineteen times to appease Slender Man, like to prove they were his followers.
ERIS: Who is Slender Man?
REBECCA: A fictional character from the internet. A tall guy in a suit with no face. He sometimes has tentacles coming out of his back.
FEY: Creepypasta.
LIAM: I watched way too many Slender Man videos in Year Two and it messed me up.
AMELIA: Are you a disciple of Slender Man?
LIAM: No.

CHRIS: And you're not going to murder us, right?
LIAM: No.
CHRIS: So all g then.
AMELIA: Did you know one of the Slender Man murderers was released? And the victim said if she ever met her again she would 'thank' her because the attack inspired her to like become a doctor! Isn't that psycho?

> ERIS *executes a brisk gesture, which has a horror sound accompanying it. This goes unnoticed by the teens.*

REBECCA: Oh shit, Mille! You're bleeding! Eurgh! Someone help her, I can't, I hate blood!

> AMELIA *realises there is blood running down her leg. She freaks out because she thinks one of her cuts has started bleeding and she doesn't want anyone to find out about them.*

FEY: Did you scratch yourself running through the bush?
AMELIA: No. It's nothing! I'm fine!
FEY: I've got a tissue if you need.
AMELIA: I'm fine, thanks! Don't come near me!
REBECCA: [*peeking a bit then hiding her face again*] That's a lotta blood for a scratch! It's dripping on the ground!
CHRIS: Ah. Amelia … Might you … have your period?
LIAM: I'm going to head over here for a bit.

> LIAM *hangs out a few metres away.*

AMELIA: I don't have my period yet.
CHRIS: You might have it now. Do you have any cramps?
AMELIA: Yeah, a bit.
CHRIS: I think you've got your period.
REBECCA: Wow, I didn't know you hadn't got it yet.
AMELIA: I don't control my own body!
CHRIS: It's cool. Happens to the best of us. Or not! No judgement.
FEY: Yeah, absolutely! Here, take these tissues and put them in your undies.

> FEY *holds out the tissues and* AMELIA *just stares at her. Eventually, she reaches out and takes them. She goes off to fix herself up.*

> ERIS *presses the blood into the ground with her foot.*

THE INITIATION

CHRIS: Liam! You can come back now! Period talk is over!

LIAM returns.

REBECCA: I love how you're completely freaked out about periods.

LIAM: I'm cool with the concept of periods, but you know. Just wanted to give Amelia some space. Isn't it special to have your first period?

REBECCA: Probably in the olden days.

CHRIS: No seriously, some people throw parties and you don't know what it's for until a special period cake comes out! Like all red and juicy!

They all respond to that image.

FEY: We should celebrate it though. We should be more positive about these things.

REBECCA: Yay! My pussy's bleeding!

ERIS: What is 'pussy'?

FEY: A vagina. Actually cunt is the more affirmative word but everyone freaks out if you say it.

CHRIS: Ooh! Next level Fey Chrysler saying the c-word!

LIAM: Yeah, I probably wouldn't say it.

AMELIA: [*returning*] Who said cunt?

FEY: Me. The etymology of the word is actually—

ERIS: Why did you all use an image of your own bodies to shame Liam?

REBECCA: What now?

CHRIS: Pussy.

LIAM: It's fine.

ERIS: You diminish yourselves in order to diminish another.

Pause: no-one has anything to say.

I love it. Let's go.

SCENE 6

Time jumps back to the end of FEY*'s monologue.* FEY *has some kind of standing seizure.*

REBECCA: Fey? Fey, are you okay?

FEY recovers. She holds The Knife in the form of a meat cleaver.

FEY: What?

CHRIS: You were just standing there babbling. Like, we couldn't understand you.
REBECCA: Are you okay? She might be having a stroke.
FEY: What? I'm fine.
AMELIA: Why does she have a knife?

> FEY *realises she is holding a meat cleaver. It is The Knife.*

FEY: Who put this here?
CHRIS: Fey, we think you're unwell. You looked like you were having a fit just now.
FEY: What? I was just …
REBECCA: It was like possession, Fey. Your eyes were rolled back …
AMELIA: Don't go near her! The knife!
ERIS: She'll be okay.
FEY: Liam! Did you put this here?
LIAM: That's not mine, that's a cleaver, like full insane clown meat cleaver. Mine's right—Shit.
CHRIS: They're not the same knife.
AMELIA: [*to* LIAM] What?
LIAM: It's gone.
CHRIS: Liam has a machete. Veeeeeery different kind of knife.
LIAM: Had.
FEY: What?
LIAM: Had a machete. It's not here anymore.
REBECCA: Fey, I think you should sit down and give me the knife.
FEY: I'm fine!
ERIS: She's fine.
FEY: I just don't know how I got this. I was telling you guys about going to therapy and my therapist asked me—
REBECCA: We couldn't understand you.
AMELIA: You were legit like …

> AMELIA *acts out a fit, her eyes rolled back, babbling.*

REBECCA: Millie!
AMELIA: And now she's waving a knife around?
FEY: Oh my god. Oh my god.
CHRIS: Maybe put the knife down.
FEY: Who put it here? Why would you do that?

REBECCA: It's okay, Fey. We didn't see you pick it up that's all. You can give me the knife and—
FEY: [*screaming*] Get it away from me!

    FEY *throws it away.*

ERIS: No!

    Everyone freezes.

AMELIA: What do you mean, no? Did you give her the knife? What is this?
ERIS: [*looking at* AMELIA *hard*] It's not my knife. But we need it.
CHRIS: Why?
FEY: I don't get why you guys couldn't understand me.
REBECCA: It's okay. Maybe we should go back.
ERIS: We can't go back.
REBECCA: Fey's sick, we have to take her back.
ERIS: No, I told you, we cannot go back until the ritual is finished.
REBECCA: Uh, I think Fey is more important than some stupid ritual.
ERIS: You can try, but the way is closed. You can't get back until we're done.
CHRIS: What do you mean, the way is closed?
ERIS: We need The Knife. We need to do the ritual.
LIAM: So we are killing something? I don't know if that's—
FEY: Becca, I'm fine.
AMELIA: You weren't fine.
ERIS: She is fine. I understood her. Why didn't any of you?
REBECCA: What are you talking about?
ERIS: Fey, didn't you say … when you're almost falling asleep you hear a voice.
FEY: Yes! See? That's what I said.
AMELIA: We … did not hear that. Right?
REBECCA: Yeah, you were just …
CHRIS: We legit couldn't understand you.
ERIS: You are just all closed to hearing what she says. And I agree with you, Fey.
CHRIS: What about?
ERIS: Everyone is going to die.
AMELIA: What the fuck??
FEY: Not tonight, I just meant eventually.
REBECCA: Yeah but what does she mean?

ERIS: [*shrugging*] The same.
LIAM: This is getting scary. Maybe we should just go home.
ERIS: We can't. The way—
CHRIS: The way is closed.
REBECCA: Fuck this. I'm taking her home.
ERIS: Do it. You will not get there and we will meet again.
REBECCA: She's fucking insane. C'mon Fey.

> FEY *and* REBECCA *exit.*

LIAM: I'm going too. Thanks for … and sorry …

> *He follows them.*

CHRIS: We should probably go.
AMELIA: Yeah, it sucks, but …
ERIS: We cannot. Try it, you will end up back here. Or, you can come and help me find The Knife.
CHRIS: Why is the knife so important to you?
ERIS: [*about* AMELIA] She knows.
AMELIA: Chris, let's just go.
CHRIS: What does she mean?
AMELIA: I have no idea. She's batshit. Let's go.
CHRIS: You're not coming?
ERIS: Come with me. This way.

> *Pause.*

CHRIS: Yeah, nah.

> ERIS *leaves coldly.*

> CHRIS *watches her go.*

CHRIS: Actually, I'm gonna go with her.

> *She follows* ERIS *to spy on her.*

AMELIA: Chris?? Fuck!

> AMELIA *reaches for The Knife for comfort and suddenly realises it's gone. She panics and searches all her pockets, looks around her. It's really gone.*

AMELIA: Fuck!

> *She runs after* REBECCA, FEY, *and* LIAM.

SCENE 7

ERIS *marches coldly through the bush.*
CHRIS *follows her, hiding as she goes.*

ERIS: [*to The Knife*] Where are you? Stop playing games! They're idiots, it'll take all night if you elude me like this!

If you're waiting for me to apologise, then I will. And you know I hate to apologise!

I'm sorry I stranded us here. I'm sorry I was soft. I'm sorry I was ever interested in humanity! Come back, let's slay!

You know you'll perish if you're not back by daybreak! Yes, I cast the spell! Surely you're not willing to be destroyed over a silly disagreement! What's even the fight? Okay you slipped away when I got obsessed with the strife here, that was immature, but now to keep yourself hidden when we're so close?

Think how well it will be to return to my sisters! The quick-tongued nine, opinions about everything which does not concern them. Endlessly tall older sisters, all in agreement, a wall of judgement. They never stop talking. I miss them.

They said I was unrealistic. I was! They said I shouldn't stay here. I should have listened! I know you're angry, but wound me and you wound yourself!

Don't be a fool, get yourself into the right hands and let's go!

CHRIS *takes out her notebook and steps on a twig, which cracks.*

ERIS: So you came with after all.

Silence.

I'm talking to you! In the bush over there!

CHRIS *doesn't move.*

Crystal, is it? Or Christine? Or … Crystalline?

CHRIS *awkwardly clambers out of the bush.*

CHRIS: Yeah, Crystal.
ERIS: I like shiny things.
CHRIS: Yeah okay. Who were you talking to?

ERIS: Why were you following me?
CHRIS: I figured we'd better not split up. Safety in numbers.
ERIS: What about all the other times? It's pretty obvious, you know.
CHRIS: What other times?
ERIS: [*touching the closed notebook*] Thirteenth of October, Person Of Interest walks into Lake Burley Griffin, singing. Melody—unfamiliar. You're obviously—
CHRIS: What?
ERIS: In love with me.
CHRIS: Um. That's really flattering that you would think that but I'm kinda straight. I'm totally cool with whatever your sexuality is—it obviously involves blood sacrifice or something so maybe not entirely cool with your sexuality—but yeah, I'm not into girls.
ERIS: Then why are you stalking me?
CHRIS: Amateur private detective.
ERIS: Why me?
CHRIS: You're … weird?
ERIS: You're weird.
CHRIS: Fair.
ERIS: You feel nothing when I touch you?

She touches Chris in a sly but tender way.

CHRIS: Stone cold straight girl.
ERIS: How annoying.

They stare at each other for a moment and then ERIS *stalks off.*

CHRIS *lets out the ragged breath she's been holding. She follows.*

SCENE 8

Time jumps back and they're all back at the beginning of the trail.

CHRIS: Okay, who hasn't had a turn? Millie! Go! Never have I ever …
REBECCA: Been chill.

    FEY *laughs.*

    During her inner monologue, the rest of the teens disappear.

AMELIA: Never have I ever … shoplifted—oh shit, yes I have! Princess Peach figurine, I will cherish you forever. Never have I ever … pierced

... no ... punched ... Oh I've definitely done that. Never! Have! I ever! ... been to a slumber party. Broken a bone. Been to church. Made a prank call. Told someone else's secret. Brushed my hair one hundred times before bed. Never have I ever made my mum proud. Never have I ever given a shit what teachers think about me. Never have I ever wanted a house and a car and a husband and two kids.

She's ready to do it for real now.

Never have I ever ... had a best friend.

She looks around to give REBECCA *a scathing look. There's no-one there.*

Shit.

Okay, real funny guys! You can come out now! You got me. I'm a little baby all alone in the woods with no friends and no-one to save me! Boo fucking hoo! I guess I'll just have to sit here and sacrifice myself to the evil creatures of darkness! Come and get me, I'm ready to be devoured!

Seriously! Don't be a bunch of little bitches, come out! I can hear you!

Fuck you all!

Fuck.

She sees something familiar a little way off. She stumbles over. It's a tiny fort made of sticks.

Oh my god, cool. Becca! I've found a fort! Just like the one we made when we were in Year Six! Exactly like the one we made in Year Six. But that was over the other side of the lake ...

She finds a detail that proves the fort is that exact fort.

What the fuuuuuuck? This is our fort. Millie plus Becca for-eva. And the cigarette box is still here. Our primary school drug stash! Empty. Just like it was ...

Becca! Stop hiding and come here!

Year Six REBECCA *appears.*

REBECCA: Sorry! Just had to give Mike a wedgie and then he had to chase me and ... well, he had no idea what to do when he caught me! Guess what?

AMELIA: What?

REBECCA: I got my period today.

AMELIA: I know.

REBECCA: How?

AMELIA: You came back from the bathroom and whispered something to Beth and Josie. You looked embarrassed, melting in your seat. Beth jumped up and went to the teacher while Josie held your hand. There was the electricity of SOMETHING HAPPENING and the whole class crackled with it. The teacher spoke to you and it made you smile and blush and she sent the three of you to the front office together. I could hear your voices in the hall: excited, urgent, hushed voices. I knew what it was.

REBECCA: Do you think the whole class knew?

AMELIA: Nah, they're all idiots.

She takes out The Knife and starts whittling with it.

REBECCA: So? Do I look different?

AMELIA: No ... What's it like?

REBECCA: I dunno, wet ... I didn't like looking at the blood, you know I hate blood. I didn't have any cramps so that's good. Can you tell I'm wearing a pad?

AMELIA: No. So is that why you wanted to meet here?

REBECCA: Nope! I've got two surprises for you! First! I got you this really cute top, just like the one Josie has.

She gives AMELIA *a tiny pale pink top with baby angels on it.*

AMELIA: Not really my style.

REBECCA: Don't be a bitch. You'll look so cute in it. You should wear it and hang out with us! You'll like them, they're really nice.

AMELIA: Doubt it.

REBECCA: Second ... this!

She holds up a slightly crushed cigarette box.

There's one left. I found it in the side of the couch, Mum forgot about it, I guess. Want to smoke it?

AMELIA: Yeah, alright.

They light it awkwardly. They both cough terribly but are loving it.

We're still best friends, right?

REBECCA: For-evaaaaa.
AMELIA: Let's do a blood pact. I read it in a book. Look, we cut ourselves here [*the palm*] and then put them together and our blood mixes. Then we're best friends for life for real.

She cuts her palm abruptly before REBECCA *knows what's happening.*

REBECCA: Millie! Don't! I can't deal with blood, you know I can't deal with blood! Don't be such a weirdo!

She runs away.

AMELIA *watches the blood pool in her palm and lets it drip onto the ground. This is the first time she has ever cut herself.*

SCENE 9

Time jumps forward: FEY, LIAM, *and* AMELIA *wander through the bush.*

AMELIA: So did you drop the knife?
LIAM: I guess so. I really don't remember, it was suddenly just gone.
AMELIA: But you don't remember anyone taking it …
LIAM: No. The weird thing is, I swear I had it right up until I didn't.
FEY: That's how it always goes. Things make sense until they don't.
AMELIA: Like you.
FEY: Was I really …
AMELIA: Babbling. Yeah.
LIAM: Full seizure, except standing.
FEY: I swear I was talking normally. And Eris understood me! How does that work?
AMELIA: That bitch is a freak. She basically kidnapped Chris just now.
LIAM: What?
AMELIA: Chris was all like, Let's go, then Eris said, Come with me, and left, then Chris WENT.
FEY: She never does what she doesn't want to do.
AMELIA: Yeah, but … She didn't seem quite like herself.
FEY: And you just left her there?
AMELIA: She ran off! And I decided to go with you guys seeing as you're a billion times less psycho.

FEY: Should we go back?
LIAM: We'll never find them.
FEY: We could try.
AMELIA: I guess. What's the worst that could happen?
LIAM: Please do not ask that question. There's plenty of worst things that could happen and as soon as we say them, they will definitely happen.
AMELIA: Okay, now I'm thinking of some pretty scary shit.

>*They all think of scary shit.*

FEY: We need to go back.
AMELIA: That's just what Eris said though, right? We'll meet again? She wanted to separate us and kill us one by one. She's probably waiting for us with machete in one hand and cleaver in the other! Chris already has her throat slit—
FEY: Stop!!
LIAM: Shit, shit, shit shit, shit—
AMELIA: Where's Rebecca?

>*They are all silent in shock.*

LIAM: Oh shit, this is how it happens.

SCENE 10

REBECCA *is on her own in the bush. She's not afraid but still trying to figure out where everyone is.*

REBECCA: Hey! Where are you guys? Well, fuck you too.

>*She is already holding The Knife in the form of a steak knife, but the audience cannot see that.*

SEB: [*voiceover*] Hey.

>*The scene melts into a different scene for* REBECCA. *She is back at* FEY's *house, in the kitchen.*

REBECCA: Oh my god Seb, you scared me.
SEB: [*voiceover*] Yeah, I'm so scary.
REBECCA: Nah, I just meant, I didn't realise you were there. Whatchu up to?
SEB: [*voiceover*] Watching a movie.

REBECCA: Yeah, we can hear it. Horror?
SEB: [*voiceover*] Slasher ... So you're eavesdropping on me.
REBECCA: Not really. Just, you know, the screams are pretty loud. What's it about?
SEB: [*voiceover*] These sorority bitches are getting slaughtered by an insane murderer. You know.
REBECCA: The usual.
SEB: [*voiceover*] Ha. Yeah.
REBECCA: Well, I better get back to Fey—
SEB: [*voiceover*] You're really pretty.
REBECCA: Uh, thanks.
SEB: [*voiceover*] Do you think you're pretty?
REBECCA: Not really.
SEB: [*voiceover*] You are. You've got a really great body. I mean, from what I can see.
REBECCA: Haha. Thanks.
SEB: [*voiceover*] ... I think about you sometimes.
REBECCA: Uh ...
SEB: [*voiceover*] Do you know what I mean?
REBECCA: I think so.
SEB: [*voiceover*] Have you ever been with someone?
REBECCA: No.
SEB: [*voiceover*] But you want to, right?
REBECCA: I guess so.
SEB: [*voiceover*] I'm just gonna get a glass from up there. You stay right there.

> REBECCA *is pinned against the kitchen bench while an invisible* SEB *presses his body against her. She is freaking out, but is frozen in place.*

Can you feel it?
REBECCA: Yes.
SEB: [*voiceover*] Do you like it?
REBECCA: Uh ...
SEB: [*voiceover*] You like it.

> REBECCA *raises her arm and it is suddenly clear she is holding* The Knife.

Don't tell anyone.

> REBECCA *screams and plunges The Knife into* FEY *who has just appeared, looking for her.*

SCENE 11

FEY *is stabbed through the gut and pinned to the tree behind her.*
REBECCA *runs off, terrified.*
FEY *can't speak, she is focussed on understanding what is happening to her—the pain, the stuckness, whether she can breathe.*
ERIS *appears.*

FEY: [*struggling to speak*] Help me.

> ERIS *places her hand on* FEY*'s forehead. It appears tender, she wipes tears from* FEY*'s cheeks.*

Help. Eris.

> ERIS *ignores her and swiftly collects her sweat and throws both the tears and sweat into the ground. She stalks off.*

Eris. Help me. Becca! Chris. I'm—I'm stuck.

> *She starts to babble in the way the other teens described earlier.*
>
> *Suddenly a new voice emerges from her. It does not sound like Fey's voice.*

THROUGH FEY: Don't be afraid.

> *She babbles fearfully in response to this and the voice speaks again.*

Don't be afraid. You are not alone.

> FEY *quietens and calms.*

Strife's key will be taken and turned.

> *The Knife slips out of the tree and the wound.*
>
> FEY *holds it lightly in her hands and pulls up her bloodied shirt: no wound.*
>
> *The light goes, all except for Telstra Tower still lit up.*

SCENE 12

Darkness.

Time jumps back to REBECCA *alone.*

SEB: [*voiceover*] Don't tell anyone.

    REBECCA *screams and plunges The Knife into a tree.*

    FEY, AMELIA, *and* LIAM *burst out through the bush, catching up to* REBECCA. *She is distressed but hides it as soon as they speak to her.*

FEY: Becca! Oh my god! Are you okay?

AMELIA: Where is she? Which way did she go?

REBECCA: I'm good. All good. I was just downstairs getting a drink. I thought you were in the kitchen. No big deal.

FEY: What are you talking about?

LIAM: We heard a scream.

REBECCA: I was just downstairs—

AMELIA: Becca, we're on Black Mountain.

REBECCA: What? Duh. Where were you guys?

FEY: She said that exact same thing earlier tonight. You said that, remember? Just before we snuck out? That's creepy. Word for word, you literally said all of that.

REBECCA: You calling me predictable, bitch?

FEY: No, I mean … What's going on with you?

AMELIA: Was Eris here? Have you seen Chris?

LIAM: There's a knife!

REBECCA: What?

FEY: Oh my god, oh my god, oh my god.

LIAM: There's a knife sticking out of this tree.

AMELIA: So she was here!

FEY: [*starting to remember*] I was … right here.

REBECCA: Ohhhh no. I thought it was a bad dream. You know how your mind wanders sometimes and then you're back where you were but you can't remember how you got there? I had a knife in my hand, in the dream. I—I don't know how it got there!

FEY: Don't be afraid.

She lifts her shirt again to check if she has a gut wound.

LIAM: It's a new knife.

AMELIA: What?

LIAM: Like, not a machete, not a cleaver.

REBECCA: Fey, I think I did something. We have to go back and make sure Seb's okay. Fey! We have to go!

FEY: Seb? What?

AMELIA: Who's Seb?

FEY: My brother. What do you mean, Becca? What did you do?

REBECCA: I didn't mean to! I didn't know I even did anything until now. I thought it was a bad dream, or, or, just how your mind goes places. But there's a real knife. I think … I think …

FEY: Becca! What are you talking about? He's fine.

REBECCA: He wouldn't leave me alone, I mean, I didn't know how to leave. I should have just left. But I didn't know what to do and then I was holding the knife—I think I—I think I stabbed—

FEY: Becca, Seb's fine. I saw him through the window as we left. He was sneaking one of my dad's beers from the laundry. He's fine. Annoying but fine.

REBECCA: Oh.

LIAM: And there's no blood.

AMELIA: What do you mean, he wouldn't leave you alone?

REBECCA: Nothing. I just got in the way.

AMELIA: What did he do?

REBECCA: He didn't do anything. I just had a weird bad dream.

LIAM: You're awake though.

AMELIA: Becca, what did that fucked up pig—

REBECCA: Stop making a big deal out of everything!

FEY: Yeah, stop saying shit about my brother!

REBECCA: Exactly. You don't know what you're talking about, Amelia.

LIAM: Don't forget about the creepy knife randomly sticking out of a tree in the middle of nowhere! The third creepy knife we've seen!

CHRIS *and* ERIS *enter.*

AMELIA: There you are!

REBECCA: We found another knife.

LIAM: It's a steak knife. Definitely not a machete or a cleaver.
ERIS: It's a shapeshifter.
CHRIS: Yeah lol, a magic shapeshifting knife.
ERIS: Something happened to you? Something was at stake.
AMELIA: Fey's brother has obviously done something—
FEY: Seriously!
LIAM: Rebecca said she hallucinated or something and stabbed the knife into the tree.
CHRIS: What did you see?
REBECCA: Can we just move on? Let's do this ritual.
FEY: I thought you weren't into it.
REBECCA: I'm bored.
ERIS: We'll need The Knife.
REBECCA: I'm not touching it.
FEY: Me neither.
CHRIS: No such thing as magic knives, people! I'll take it.
ERIS: [*holding* CHRIS *back*] No. Who owns it? You.
LIAM: Me? No. I had the machete. This is clearly a steak knife.
ERIS: Doesn't matter what knife it is, we just need a knife. It's your initiation so you bring The Knife. Pull it from the tree, let's go.
LIAM: Let's just leave it. It's creepy.
ERIS: We need it.
LIAM: Someone else take it.
REBECCA: You are the Man, Liam.
LIAM: Aw fine! As long as you don't start that again. I'm really regretting all of this.

He marches up to The Knife but as soon as he touches it, it triggers his fears and he has a full-blown panic attack.

Everyone is freaked out but REBECCA *moves in to comfort him with a touch on the shoulder. He lashes out.*

Back off, bitch!

REBECCA *keeps it together.*

AMELIA *knows what it is like to have a panic attack.*

AMELIA: Liam. Hold your breath then let it out slowly.
LIAM: I can't—Ican'tbreathe—I—

AMELIA: Hold your breath. Let it out slowly. Good. Now, tell me five things you can see.
LIAM: I—I can't—
CHRIS: Trees.
FEY: Rocks.
LIAM: Grass.
AMELIA: Good, two more.
LIAM: You guys. The moon.
AMELIA: Tell me four things you can feel, like, touch.
LIAM: Leaves. Sticks.

He almost starts to panic again but keeps trying to focus on the task.

Dirt! And ... the air.
AMELIA: Tell me three things you can hear.
LIAM: Insects. The wind ... Trees.
AMELIA: Two things you can smell.
LIAM: Eucalyptus. The earth.
AMELIA: And one thing you can taste.

LIAM has calmed down enough to make a joke.

LIAM: Uh, my own snot.

Everyone laughs with relief.

Sorry. So embarrassing.
CHRIS: S'all good.
LIAM: This ... actually happens a lot. I don't know why. Anytime I feel out of control ... But I was fine and then—
REBECCA: You touched the knife.
FEY: And you had that hallucination—
REBECCA: When I was holding the knife.
LIAM: I was fine before when I had the machete. It actually made me feel better.
CHRIS: They're not the same knife, guys.
ERIS: The knife gives you what you need.
AMELIA: A panic attack?
ERIS: Someone to help you out of your panic. We're almost there, at the place of initiation. Are you ready, Liam?
LIAM: Weirdly, I am. No blood shed or sex stuff though. Right?

ERIS: We'll see. Keep going down there.

> LIAM, AMELIA, FEY, *and* REBECCA *exit down the path.*

Take it.
CHRIS: Why don't you?
ERIS: Does it belong to you?
CHRIS: No. It's yours, isn't it?
ERIS: Not yet.
CHRIS: So take it then. You're obviously obsessed with it.
ERIS: Obsessed?
CHRIS: Can't stop talking about it. Think about it all the time. Every turn you make, you hope it will be there. Watch for it, wait for it. Bide your time. Lay your traps. I can't stop talking.
ERIS: Take The Knife.

> CHRIS *wants to make* ERIS *take it but suddenly she feels compelled to take The Knife herself. They are looking at each other, can't look away. She tries to resist but cannot.*

CHRIS: I don't want to.
ERIS: Then why are you reaching for it?
CHRIS: I don't know.
ERIS: Then stop.
CHRIS: I can't. You take it.
ERIS: Why do you want me to so much?
CHRIS: I want to see what it turns into when you touch it.
ERIS: That's not rational.
CHRIS: I know.
ERIS: You only believe in what's rational.
CHRIS: I know.
ERIS: And yet …

> CHRIS *pulls The Knife from the tree and it transforms into a pearl-handled switchblade.*
>
> ERIS *holds Chris' hands steady without touching The Knife.*

I've never seen it take this form.
CHRIS: A switchblade. Mother-of-pearl handle.
ERIS: It's beautiful.
CHRIS: Feels good to hold.

ERIS: The knife wants to be held. The knife wants to be beheld.

> ERIS *turns swiftly and exits.*
>
> CHRIS *hides The Knife. No-one will make her do anything.*

SCENE 13

REBECCA *steps into a clearing away from the group.* LIAM *follows.*

LIAM: You okay?

> REBECCA *jumps with fright but relaxes when she sees it's* LIAM.

REBECCA: Are *you* okay? That was a full-on panic attack back there.
LIAM: Not very manly, panic attacks.
REBECCA: Fuck manly.
LIAM: Yeah, I guess. Amelia is really protective of you, hey?
REBECCA: Yeah. That's basically why we can't be friends anymore. In Year Six, she would beat the shit out of anyone who looked at me wrong. Not cool.

> *Pause.*

LIAM: Was she right about that dude?
REBECCA: What dude?
LIAM: Fey's brother.
REBECCA: I dunno.
LIAM: What did he do?
REBECCA: Why? So you can take notes and learn how to be a man?
LIAM: More like the opposite.

> *Beat.*

REBECCA: I can't really tell what was wrong and what was fine. Like, we were chatting, and he is hot but—sorry this is making me feel a bit sick …
LIAM: You don't have to—
REBECCA: Nah. It's good. We need to talk about these things. Especially creeps. Don't be a creep, ey?
LIAM: Noted.
REBECCA: It's hard to talk about because like, when did it turn into a bad situation? And he said I was pretty, which of course I like,

but in a creepy way, which I don't like? Or was it actually creepy? I can't tell. It's the way he looks at me. But it's not a crime to look at people, right? But then he sorta pinned me against the kitchen bench but he didn't hurt me or anything but I was kinda freaking out … I guess I'm not ready for … I don't even know.

LIAM: Yeah, I know. I'm not ready for anything.

REBECCA: It's like, I just want to grow up without an audience! I feel people looking at me all the time and it's like they have all these ideas about me which I don't even get.

LIAM: If you were Medusa then if people looked at you they'd turn to stone.

REBECCA: Yeah! And I'd have all my snaky girls to chill with.

LIAM: And your blood is so potent, when they cut your head off, Pegasus is born from the spot where the blood drips.

REBECCA: Yeah, maybe don't visualise my decapitation.

LIAM: How else will we defeat the Chimera?

REBECCA: The what now?

LIAM: Part-lion, part-goat, part-snake, breathes fire. Yeah, I know: nerd. But seriously though—

REBECCA: Seriously!

LIAM: You know what Eris means?

REBECCA: What?

LIAM: Strife. She's the goddess of strife and discord.

REBECCA: Sucks to be her. My name means to bind or to snare: fuck yeah.

LIAM: Becca, I think she actually is the goddess Strife.

REBECCA: O-kayyyyy …

LIAM: We need to be careful. Something is happening. We might … need to kill her.

There's the howl of a beast in the distance.

SCENE 14

They are back in the bush together. The Knife is stuck in the tree.

ERIS: Doesn't matter what knife it is, we just need a knife. It's your initiation so you bring The Knife. Pull it from the tree, let's go.

LIAM: Let's just leave it. It's creepy.
ERIS: We need it.
LIAM: Someone else take it.
REBECCA: You are the Man, Liam.
LIAM: Aw fine! As long as you don't start that again. I'm really regretting all of this.

> *He marches up to The Knife and grasps it but he can't pull it free.*

ERIS: Take The Knife, Liam.
LIAM: Hang on. It's really stuck in there.
CHRIS: Try wiggling it a bit. It'll loosen it up.
LIAM: It's not budging. How'd you even get it in here so deep?
REBECCA: I guess I'm super buff when I'm freaking out.
AMELIA: Let me try!
LIAM: No, I've got it. If I just …

> *He uses all of his weight to try and pull it, but it resists.*

CHRIS: Maybe if you—
FEY: Let's cheer him on: Be a Man! Be a Man!

> *The chant continues as the other teens join in.*

ERIS: Come on, Liam. Pull The Knife!
LIAM: I'm trying!

> *He uses a foot against the tree to brace himself. And then the other. The Knife doesn't move.*

What the heck?
ERIS: Be a man, Liam! Don't let a little knife get the better of you!
LIAM: Guys, shut up! I've got this!
ERIS: Pull The Knife, Liam!
CHRIS: [*moving forward to help*] Here, let me have a go.
LIAM: No, I want to do it!

> *He pushes* CHRIS *aside and she falls.*

> ERIS *makes a supernatural gesture and* LIAM *is strung up by invisible ropes.*

ERIS: Don't touch her.

> LIAM *is terrified and pisses himself.*

AMELIA: Is that ... ?
CHRIS: Eris, I'm fine.
ERIS: Liam, you're pissing yourself. In front of us all.
CHRIS: Eris, stop.

> LIAM *tries to speak but his mouth is stopped by the magic.*

ERIS: You're not a man after all. Just a little dog, pissing himself when he gets scared. Sit.

> LIAM *sits like a dog. He tries to speak but cannot and it starts to sound like the grunts of an animal.*

Good boy. Lie down. In your own piss.

> LIAM *obeys but desperately doesn't want to.*

Now. Get lost. We don't need you anymore.

> *She releases him from the magic and he runs off like a wild beast, howling.*

Someone pull The Knife and let's go.

> *No-one moves.*

> ERIS *looks at* CHRIS *and she immediately retrieves The Knife easily from the tree and they all follow* ERIS *further into the bush.*

SCENE 15

LIAM, *as the beast, hurtles into a clearing. He is muddy and has cuts.*

He curls up and licks his wounds for a moment.

He sits up and tries to speak. He can only make the sounds of a beast. He tries really hard to speak, but cannot.

He howls with frustration.

He has the senses of a beast and can hear the others in the distance. He can smell them.

He is hungry. He wants to hunt.

He readies himself, howls with determination, and runs off into the bush.

SCENE 16

Everyone is there. LIAM *is not a beast, but his pants are still wet.* FEY's *torso is bloody, etc. These things go unacknowledged.*

ERIS: This is the place. Chris, put The Knife on the altar.
CHRIS: I don't have it.
ERIS: You just pulled it from the tree.
CHRIS: Yeah, and I hid it. Knives are dangerous! We don't need that hanging over our heads.
ERIS: [*storming off towards The Knife*] This is your fault! And you will perish if you don't come back!
CHRIS: I think now is the time to present my research on her.
LIAM: Research?
CHRIS: I've been following her for weeks. She's … weird.
AMELIA: We all know that.
CHRIS: No, I mean, she's *weird*. Listen to this.

She pulls out her detective notebook.

REBECCA: What the fuck is that?
CHRIS: Uh, Becca, this is a NOTEBOOK. Okay. August seventeenth … POI—Person of Interest—sits in the foodcourt for an hour and everyone who walks past spills their food. October tenth, traffic lights malfunction as she crosses the road: all green. October twelfth, POI stands in Haynes Street staring at number thirty-three, just staring at the house and—
AMELIA: That's my house!
CHRIS: Interesting!
AMELIA: Oh shit. Why is she staring at my house?
CHRIS: And muttering.
AMELIA: Muttering! What?
CHRIS: Couldn't get close enough.
AMELIA: Oh my god.
FEY: This is creepy … Keep going!
CHRIS: And tonight—
AMELIA: Um! She knows where I live. Can we focus on that?
CHRIS: I was following her and I saw her do this weird thing. Actually, it was just outside the window you guys climbed out of.

FEY: WHAT?
REBECCA: What did she do?
CHRIS: She was eating a toffee apple, and then she said this creepy rhyme, you know, 'Apple on a stick, it makes me sick … '
AMELIA: Makes my heart beat—
CHRIS: Yeah. She did the whole rhyme, scratched my name into the ground, and she stabbed *this* in the middle of it all.

She pulls out the baggie with a flourish, but it's empty.

Crap. [*Checking her pockets*] It's gone!
FEY: What was it?
CHRIS: The stick. Of the toffee apple. Crap. I must've … dropped it? But the bag is still here and sealed …
REBECCA: Why did she write your name?
AMELIA: I think she's a witch. She must have been doing a spell. She's bewitched us and she's going to kill us and use our guts for some fucked up magic. Why did we come here?
LIAM: Shit, shit, shit, shit—
REBECCA: Calm down. Guys. There's five of us, one of her. She's a spindly little bitch, we can take her. She's not a witch, they don't exist.
FEY: Actually it is a legit spirituality.
REBECCA: Okay yeah, but not like cutting up children in the forest. She ate an apple and did a rhyme. Calm the fuck down.
CHRIS: I agree. Not a witch, just weird.
REBECCA: Why are you so obsessed with her?
CHRIS: I'm not obsessed, I just—
REBECCA: You are so completely obsessed.
CHRIS: It's my hobby, private investigation. Nerdy, yes, but not obsessed.
FEY: Why are you following her?
CHRIS: The first time I saw her, I was studying at the library next to one of those big windows and I looked up and she was standing outside, staring right at me.
LIAM: Those windows are mirrors on the outside. You can't see in through them.
CHRIS: Exactly. She was far away so I didn't really think anything about it. But then she came up to the window.

AMELIA: Creepy.
CHRIS: I just thought it was going to be funny, like you know how people fix their make up in the window or make sure there's nothing in their teeth?
LIAM: People are always checking themselves out there.
CHRIS: So I thought it'd be hilarious and she'd like squeeze a pimple or something.
REBECCA: Ew.
CHRIS: But she just kept looking at me. Even though I knew she couldn't see through, it really felt like she could see me. My heart was beating so fast, I felt sick. And I was just about to get up and leave and she spun around and left. Then I kept seeing her around and so I sorta started following her.
REBECCA: Wow, you are completely gay for Eris.
CHRIS: What? Shut the hell up.

SCENE 17

Nightmare scene: the teens surround REBECCA *in some way and perform the chant. She thinks it's the game—she's done most of the ones that make sense but as the chant goes on, she can't be sure but feels like maybe she did accidentally? She gets more and more distressed as the game progresses.*

ALL: Never have I ever
AMELIA: Made out with someone
ALL: Never have I ever
ERIS: Had a crush on a teacher
ALL: Never have I ever
FEY: Led someone on
ALL: Never have I ever
CHRIS: Come skinny dipping!
ALL: Never have I ever

    Beat.

LIAM: Send nudes
ALL: Never have I ever
FEY: Oh my god!
ALL: Never have I ever

ERIS: Do you want it to be about sex?
ALL: Never have I ever
SEB: [*voiceover*] Don't tell anyone
ALL: Never have I ever
AMELIA: I like this private school slut thing you've got going on.
ALL: Never have I ever
FEY: What are you doing?
ALL: Never have I ever
CHRIS: Becca, leave him alone!
ALL: Never have I ever
LIAM: Was she right about that dude?
ALL: Never have I ever
CHRIS: Stop making everything about sex.
ALL: Never have I ever
CHRIS: Who bullied Liam about lesbian porn?
ALL: Never have I ever
CHRIS: Who wouldn't shut up about doing a sex ritual?
ALL: Never have I ever
CHRIS: Who is obsessed with Fey's older brother?

Chant speeds up and batters REBECCA *around.*

ALL: Never have I ever
ERIS: Apple on a stick
ALL: Never have I ever
LIAM: Makes me sick
ALL: Never have I ever
CHRIS: Not because you're dirty
ALL: Never have I ever
FEY: Not because you're clean
ALL: Never have I ever
ERIS *and* CHRIS: Girls, boys
ALL: Never have I ever
AMELIA *and* FEY: Having fun
ALL: Never have I ever
AMELIA *and* CHRIS: She can wiggle, she can waggle
ALL: Never have I ever
LIAM *and* FEY: She can even do the splits

ALL: Never have I ever
ERIS: Close your eyes

>   *She gives The Knife to* REBECCA.

ALL: Never have I ever
SEB: [*voiceover*] Don't say anything

>   REBECCA *projectile vomits everywhere.*

ALL: Threesome, foursome, fivesome, sixsome, sevensome, eightsome, ninesome, tensome
AMELIA: If you muck it up then you're not my friend

>   REBECCA *cuts her own head off and falls to the ground.*

SCENE 18

CHRIS *is almost suspended in mid-air by* ERIS*'s invisible grip.*

ERIS *digs a grave in the ground.*

ERIS: It was easy to make Amelia bleed, to make Liam piss himself. Rebecca needed to expel what was stuck inside her and Fey needed to cry, to sweat it out. But to coax your heart out, to make it beat two-forty-six ... I don't know if I can. Love spells are usually so easy but I've honestly failed to cast it on you. That's why I must regrow you.

>   [*To herself*] I must have the sacrifice of the innocent, I must have the five bodily fluids shed into the ground, and I must eat from the heart of love.

CHRIS: Is that why you wrote my name on the ground? A love spell?
ERIS: Maybe that's it. Country is rejecting my magic. [*To Country*] What do you even want?
CHRIS: Maybe it didn't work because ... I already ...
ERIS: What?
CHRIS: I guess I sorta have a crush on you.
ERIS: What?
CHRIS: Maybe my first one. Which is why I didn't quite know what it was. It's not like how other people describe it. Like, I've got a crush on someone! Love-heart eyes, etc. I don't feel love-heart eyes. I feel obsessed with you, like I want to hunt you down and ... and ...
ERIS: And what?

CHRIS: I seriously have no idea. Be buried alive by you?
ERIS: You dig then!
CHRIS: You want me to dig my own grave?
ERIS: Yes.
CHRIS: To prove I have a crush on you.
ERIS: Yes.
CHRIS: Can't we just, I dunno, be girlfriends and have hot chocolates in a café?
ERIS: I'm not that kind of girl.
CHRIS: And that's why I like you. Okay, untie me.
ERIS: And you'll dig your own grave. This isn't a trick?
CHRIS: I'm not sure how I can outsmart you.

> ERIS *releases her. They are wary of each other.* CHRIS *begins to dig.*

So is this what love feels like? I mean, is a love spell the same feeling as real love? I have no point of comparison.
ERIS: What does it feel like?
CHRIS: My mind keeps tripping up on you. As I move around the world, I feel like I'm circling you. I feel hungry for you but I wouldn't know how to take a bite.
ERIS: Yeah, that's what it's like.
CHRIS: Which one? The spell or the real thing?
ERIS: They feel the same.

SCENE 19

AMELIA *stumbles around, she can't find anyone.* ERIS *is watching and fills* AMELIA *up with the very worst feelings.* AMELIA *doesn't know how to survive them.*

She instinctively reaches into her pocket for The Knife. It's not there.

She tries to find something she can use to hurt herself. The sticks break, the rocks are too blunt.

REBECCA: [*faraway voice*] Millie … Millie …

> AMELIA *slaps herself on the cheek. It's not the best but there is enough of a shock to anchor her to reality. She hits herself again. And again. As many times as she needs to feel better. And each slap is momentous.*

Then, when she has fully returned to reality, she can touch her cheek softly. She cools it with the back of her fingers.

Suddenly she can feel the presence of The Knife.

She discovers it hidden where Chris hid it. It is her dagger. She feels almost dizzy with relief.

ERIS *exits, satisdued.*

AMELIA *sits down and looks around to make sure no-one is anywhere near her.*

Then she carefully pulls up her skirt and gets ready to make a cut on her thigh next to the line of all the other cuts she has made there.

There is an unearthly sound.

She is horrified to discover The Knife has become a bone.

Millie! Is that you?
AMELIA: Becca? Where are you?
REBECCA: Down here. Don't freak out but …

AMELIA *finds her and screams.*

SCENE 20

The teens are back where they were when ERIS *stormed off for The Knife.* REBECCA *is not headless.*

CHRIS: She just kept looking at me. Even though I knew she couldn't see through, it really felt like she could see me. My heart was beating so fast, I felt sick. And I was just about to get up and leave and she spun around and left. Then I kept seeing her around and so I sorta started following her.
REBECCA: Wow, you are completely gay for Eris.
CHRIS: What? Shut the hell up.
REBECCA: You so are! How does it feel to be gay for a creepy bitch?
CHRIS: Becca, seriously, just because you can't come to terms with your own sluttiness doesn't mean you have to drag everyone about their sexuality. I'm not gay. I would know!
REBECCA: What the fuck are you talking about?
CHRIS: I'm not gay—deal with it.

REBECCA: No, you're saying I'm a slut?
FEY: Chris, not cool.
AMELIA: Yeah, don't slut-shame!
CHRIS: Fine. Sorry, Becca. But stop making everything about sex.
REBECCA: What? I don't!
CHRIS: Uh, yes you do! Who bullied Liam about lesbian porn? Who wouldn't shut up about doing a sex ritual? Who is obsessed with Fey's older brother? / You talk about him all the time.
AMELIA: Shut up, Chris.
FEY: Chris, leave her alone!
CHRIS: Don't talk about my sexuality like you know anything about it!
REBECCA: Okay! Sorry! Jeez.
CHRIS: Okay.
REBECCA: You looked happy, that's all.
CHRIS: Okay.
REBECCA: And I'm not obsessed with Seb.

Beat

He's obsessed with me and it makes me feel weird.
FEY: What?
REBECCA: He says creepy things to me sometimes. And … sort of touched me …
FEY: WHAT?
AMELIA: I KNEW IT. THAT DICKHEAD!!
REBECCA: Millie, it's fine. He just leant into me. For a second. It was confusing and sorta gross but I'm okay.
FEY: That's not okay. THAT'S NOT OKAY. I'm going to kill him. I'm really going to fucking—
REBECCA: It's probably my fault. I don't mean to be sexual but—
LIAM: It's not your fault.
AMELIA: It's definitely not your fault.
FEY: It is so not your fault!
REBECCA: Yeah, okay. Maybe.
FEY: I can't believe this!! No, no, no, no that's not what I mean: I one hundred percent believe you Becca, I just mean—my own brother is—one of those … bad guys! I feel sick.

CHRIS: [*almost in tears*] Becca, I'm so sorry. I don't know why I said those things, they were really crap things to say and so not true. I'm really sorry.
FEY: Yeah, Chris that was really fucked!
REBECCA: It's okay. I'm okay, Fey. Come here. I'm sorry too, Chris: if you're not gay, you're not gay …
CHRIS: Why would you even say that?
REBECCA: You both look really into each other. That's all. Maybe she is a witch and has you under her spell.
CHRIS: Don't believe in that crap.
REBECCA: Neither, but …
CHRIS: Maybe I am a bit obsessed.
AMELIA: Okay but why was she staring at my house? What does she want with me?
REBECCA: I guess you're next.
LIAM: Don't say it like that: you're next!
REBECCA: [*in a creepy voice*] You're NEXT.
LIAM: Stop!
REBECCA: YOU'RE NEXT!

The bush explodes into light.

SCENE 21

A menacing sound. Supernatural wind fills the stage.

ERIS *enters in full goddess form: Strife.*

REBECCA *is reduced to a severed head.*

FEY *starts having a fit again.*

CHRIS *digs her own grave.*

LIAM *is a beast stalking them in the background.*

AMELIA *holds her dagger, The Knife from the fort.*

ERIS: You are the one who owns this Knife?
AMELIA: Yes.
ERIS: Why is The Knife bound to you?
AMELIA: I don't know.
ERIS: This is not something you just don't know! If The Knife is bound to you, you know and you know why!

Holding this knowledge back will destroy you and it will destroy me and yes, even you my sharp friend.

We are almost together again, don't fail me, Knife-in-the-back! You are my companion, my familiar, you are a part of me! Remember your friendship to me!

Compel her to tell me what I need to know to work the magic! Amelia, I ask again: why is The Knife bound to you?

> AMELIA *grips The Knife and it gives her what she needs to answer. She cannot speak but she can show* ERIS. *She stretches out her arm and pulls her sleeve back: there are many cuts lined up in various stages of healing.*

Are you innocent?

> AMELIA *snakes her arm back into her sleeve and holds it defensively.*

AMELIA: No! Obviously!

ERIS: The Knife is never in the hands of the guilty.

> AMELIA *is crying.*

AMELIA: I … No! I'm not. I did this! I know it's wrong but I did it anyway. I had to do it. And I know it's wrong!

ERIS: Tell me what you are.

> *Pause.*

Knife, help her.

AMELIA: I'm … I'm … I'm … innocent.

ERIS: Will you make the sacrifice?

CHRIS: Eris, you were right!

ERIS: About what?

CHRIS: I'll give you my heart. And you can't kill Amelia.

AMELIA: Chris, no!

ERIS: Do it then.

CHRIS: You won't hurt Amelia.

ERIS: Agreed.

> ERIS *gives* CHRIS *the power to reach into her chest. With great difficulty she pulls out her actual heart and offers the bloody mass to* ERIS.

ERIS *takes a luscious bite, blood running down her chin.*

CHRIS: [*dying*] Now, you can't hurt Amelia.

ERIS: Amelia! The sacrifice. I need The Knife returned to me. It is the key to the door to my realm. It must be freely given, neither thieved nor found. You are the owner, you are the innocent, you must make the sacrifice.

REBECCA: What? You just need her to give you that knife? Chris just killed herself to protect Amelia! For nothing!

AMELIA: It doesn't want to leave me.

ERIS: Yes, in the final moment, The Knife will try to make itself irresistible to you. This is because the sacrifice must be real for the transference to work.

AMELIA: I need it.

ERIS: You need to relinquish it. The Knife gave you what you needed, now you must begin again.

AMELIA: You're powerful, you don't need it.

ERIS: I need to go home!

AMELIA *grips The Knife and decides.*

AMELIA: No.

REBECCA: Amelia!!

ERIS: I knew this would happen. So close, we found each other again AFTER THOUSANDS OF YEARS, we made magic together again but humanity is a dead end.

FEY: We're not a dead end.

ERIS: You're right. Not all of you. But it doesn't matter now, the scales have tipped and it's all strife all the time from now until humanity's end.

AMELIA: It's all I have.

Beat.

REBECCA: You have me.

FEY: You have me too.

AMELIA: You must think I'm really insane for doing this.

REBECCA: I don't understand it, Millie, but I know it's something people do …

FEY: To cope.

AMELIA: You must think I'm fucked up.

FEY: Not more than any of us.

ERIS: Make your decision.

AMELIA: I want to. I want to get rid of it. I want this out of my life. But I also can't deal without it.

REBECCA: We'll help you.

AMELIA: We're not friends anymore, remember.

FEY: We're friends now!

REBECCA: Millie, I miss you. I was a bitch. I'm sorry.

AMELIA: I miss you too. Don't feel sorry for me though! No-one!

REBECCA: No way.

FEY: It's just something people do to get through.

REBECCA: We'll help you find a new way. Give her the knife.

> AMELIA *looks at The Knife and almost can't bear to part with it. But she finds a way and offers it to* ERIS.
>
> ERIS, *so close to her thousands-years-old goal, is nervous. She slowly takes The Knife and they both glow with their reunion.*
>
> LIAM *leaps forward and attacks* ERIS *by biting her jugular. Blood is everywhere.*
>
> ERIS *cries out and she drops The Knife.*
>
> FEY *begins to have a fit again.*

THROUGH FEY: Don't be afraid.

> *With one magic gesture* ERIS *slams* LIAM *aside, killing him instantly.*
>
> *She clears her throat and holds out her hand.*

ERIS: The Knife. Now.

THROUGH FEY: It has been taken.

ERIS: What?

THROUGH FEY: Your key has been taken and turned.

> ERIS *shrieks with anger and tries to dig it up again. There's nothing there.*

ERIS: One last exchange then.

> *She looks around and she sees Telstra Tower glowing. Furious, she pulls it from the mountain and wields it as her sword.*

There is a sound of pent-up energy being released from the top of the mountain.

The landscape transforms and the lake is revealed.

ERIS *turns to the lake and plunges Telstra Tower into the lake.*

Water moves back and a portal is opened. An arm stretches out of the watery grave-like portal. It is the arm of one of Eris's sisters. It waits for her.

ERIS *looks at the bloodied teens and beckons to the sky to call forth rain.*

ERIS *finally performs the initiation ritual. As she speaks the name of each teen, they rise, become whole, transform, the rain washing blood away.*

Amelia, begin anew. No more cloak and dagger.
Rebecca, begin anew. Stake out the territory of your own pleasure.
Fey, begin anew. Cleave to or cleave apart, you must decide yourself.
Liam, begin anew. Your small kindnesses, from there you make yourself a man.
Chris …

ERIS *cannot look directly at* CHRIS. *She blinks and is discomfited at her inability to see her.*

You break the light apart for me, I … cannot see. I don't know why. This has never happened before. The Knife brought you to me and I don't know why.

CHRIS *walks up to* ERIS *and touches her.*

CHRIS: I don't want you to go.
ERIS: I want to go, I will go. Come with me.
CHRIS: Where?
ERIS: To my realm, my home.
CHRIS: I … want to.
AMELIA: Chris, you can't go! Stop doing your magic on her!
CHRIS: Millie, there's no magic. I mean, I was going to say no such thing as magic but … [*Gesturing to the arm waiting in the open lake portal*] I'm not under a spell, I'm not bewitched. I want to go with her.

LIAM: Chris, if you leave everyone will think you are dead.
FEY: Or worse, a missing person. Think about your parents, Chris! They'll go crazy.
REBECCA: No-one will believe us when we say what really happened.
AMELIA: Chris, you really really really can't go. Please.
CHRIS: If I don't go, can I ever see you again?
ERIS: You still have this.

> *She taps in the centre of Chris' ribcage.*

Apple on a stick, you make me sick.
CHRIS: You make my heart beat.

> ERIS *turns to the portal, takes the hand of her sister, she enters the portal, and leaves Earth.*

SCENE 22

Darkness. Kookaburras.

*The teens—*REBECCA, FEY, AMELIA, LIAM, *and* CHRIS*—wake up in the grassy bank at the top of David Street, back in the real world as the sun rises.*

LIAM *sees a jogger run past across the street, looking at them strangely.*

LIAM: Damn. That's my neighbour.
REBECCA: Everybody wave.

> *They all wave sleepily.*

CHRIS: Did all that actually happen? Do you guys even know what I'm talking about?
REBECCA: Cutting off my own head and shit?
CHRIS: Yeah. Did it happen?
LIAM: We can't have all dreamed the same thing.
AMELIA: What did you dream?
LIAM: We went into the bush, I found a machete.
FEY: Which turned into a meat cleaver.
LIAM: And then a steak knife, a switchblade, a dagger, and a sword.
AMELIA: Eris is actually a psycho witch.
LIAM: The goddess Strife, actually.
REBECCA: An arm came out of a fucking portal in Lake Burley Griffin.

LIAM: And Telstra Tower is—
CHRIS: She's gone.

>Beat.

AMELIA: You okay?
CHRIS: Yeah. No … A bit stunned, I guess.
FEY: So how do you live your normal life again after discovering that everything you thought wasn't real might be, and everything you believed was real might not be … ?
LIAM: And no-one will ever believe us.
REBECCA: We don't tell anyone. We don't need to. We have each other, we survived a night on Black Mountain, we've been initiated by an insane goddess, I was right about Chris being gay for Eris …
CHRIS: Wow. You waited a whole two minutes.
REBECCA: After this transformative experience, Chris, I am a new person.
AMELIA: I don't want to go back to normal.

>FEY *takes her hand.*

FEY: We can't. None of us can.

>REBECCA *takes* AMELIA*'s other hand.*

REBECCA: You have us.
AMELIA: Thanks.

>*She squeezes their hands tight because she can't say anything else.*

CHRIS: We made a bet.
REBECCA: What now?
CHRIS: Eris and I made a bet. If I gave her my heart and let her eat from it, she got whatever she wanted. And if I didn't, I got whatever I wanted.
AMELIA: We all saw you dig your own heart out and give it to her.
CHRIS: Yeah, but. It's here. So I did and I didn't.
FEY: Yeah, I was pinned to a tree by the knife through my guts but then, no wound.
LIAM: Both are true.
REBECCA: I kinda liked being a severed head.
FEY: And my brother … I feel sick about it. What are we going to do?

REBECCA: I have no idea. Kinda don't want to go back to your house.
AMELIA: Come to mine. I'll make pancakes and we can all make a plan.
REBECCA: Thanks Millie.
CHRIS: So how do I do it? Do I make a wish?
AMELIA: That is something I never thought you would say!
FEY: Ooh Chris, what do you wish for?
CHRIS: Actually, I think I need to be alone when I … wish it.
LIAM: My mum will be up soon.
AMELIA: God, I forget parents even existed.
FEY: Hey, can you see Telstra Tower? Is it still there?

> *They all turn, except* CHRIS, *searching for the sight of Telstra Tower in the misty morning.*
>
> CHRIS *looks up for a while, listening to Country.*
>
> *She gathers up her resolve.*

CHRIS: I want to see you again!

> *The stage is swallowed into darkness with a supernatural horror sound.*

THE END

CANBERRA YOUTH THEATRE PRESENTS

THE INITIATION
BY CATHY PETOCZ

WORLD PREMIERE
15 - 19 JUNE 2022
THE COURTYARD STUDIO – CANBERRA THEATRE CENTRE

CAST

REBECCA / SEB	SYLVIE BURKE
ERIS	LATSAMY CARRUTHERS
FEY	ZOE HARRIS
AMELIA	JUNIPER POTTER
CHRIS	TARA SAXENA
LIAM	HARRY ZIARNO

CREATIVE TEAM

DIRECTOR	CATHY PETOCZ
SET & COSTUME DESIGNER	NYX MATHEWS
LIGHTING DESIGNER	GILLIAN SCHWAB
SOUND DESIGNER	PATRICK HAESLER
ASSISTANT DIRECTOR	CAITLIN BAKER
STAGE MANAGER	RHILEY WINNETT
DRAMATURGY & CULTURAL SUPPORT	ETHAN BELL

ACKNOWLEDGEMENTS

Thank you to Hannah de Feyter, Anna Johnston, Aphir, Peter Matheson, Dr. Benny Wilson, Rex Rollin for set construction expertise and assistance, and artsACT for funding Ethan Bell's dramaturgical and cultural consultation during script development.

We greatly acknowledge the support of Ainslie and Gorman Arts Centres, and the ACT Government through artsACT.

This production is supported by Canberra Theatre Centre, as part of a commitment to nurturing the young and emerging artists of the ACT.

PLAYWRIGHT & DIRECTOR'S NOTES

Canberra Youth Theatre is a special company. I was a kid when I first saw a Canberra Youth Theatre performance, a collaboration between a Vietnamese water puppetry company and local young artists. Tiny First Fleet ships invaded an inflatable paddle pool, a duck puppet sailed past attached to a diver's head, and an ensemble of recorder players heralded the event. My whole body tingled with excitement: whatever this is, I want to do it too.

Now making theatre is my life's work and it is an honour to do so as part of Canberra Youth Theatre's exciting community. *The Initiation* is a play seeded within the company's semester workshop program, developed with fourteen dedicated and fearless teen actors over the last two pandemic years, and supported by Canberra Youth Theatre's visionary staff from conception through to this world premiere season. I was pleased to be awarded funding from artsACT to work with the generous and talented Ngunnawal poet Ethan Bell on the dramaturgy of the script, focussing particularly on how Country is represented in the play. Look up his poetry! I have never seen Ngunnawal Country in a text as vivid as in Ethan's poem, *Bury Me*.

As you journey through *The Initiation*'s fantastical, wild Black Mountain, remember how you feel at different moments, notice what horror-laden teen memories come up for you, and take note of what you feel drawn to, or repelled by. Then, talk! Discuss themes with your neighbour, fight with your best friend about which is the goriest bit, and tell the cast and crew which parts brought up the strongest feelings for you.

There is much to fear in the world at the moment, but I'm not afraid of the future because if it's filled with the humans who are our teen artists now, we are in brave and caring hands.

Cathy Petocz

THE VOICE OF YOUTH EXPRESSED THROUGH INTELLIGENT AND CHALLENGING THEATRE

Canberra Youth Theatre is one of the leading youth arts companies in Australia.

We create opportunities for young people to collaborate, develop their artistic skills and create pathways to the professional arts sector.

We advocate for and amplify the voices of young people, providing a space for them to discover and express their creative selves.

We produce powerful theatre where young artists ignite urgent conversations, challenge the forces that shape them, and invite us to see the world from new perspectives.

Over its 50 year history, Canberra Youth Theatre has proven experience commissioning, developing, producing and promoting new Australian writing.

From Debra Oswald's now Australian classic *Dags*, and works by writers Tommy Murphy, Mary Rachel Brown, Lachlan Philpott, Angela Betzien, Liv Hewson, Ross Mueller, Emily Sheehan, Jessica Bellamy and Tasnim Hossain, we have nurtured new voices and commissioned professional artists to create acclaimed works for young people.

Canberra Youth Theatre acknowledges the Ngunnawal people as the traditional custodians of the lands on which we collaborate, share stories and create art. We pay respect to their Elders, past and present and emerging, and recognise their enduring culture and contribution to our community. We celebrate their rich history of over 60,000 years of storytelling, and are privileged and grateful to share our stories here. This is Ngunnawal country. Always was. Always will be.

SYLVIE BURKE | REBECCA / SEB

Sylvie started acting at age 9 when she joined Drama Spot in Lane Cove, Sydney. It was there that Sylvie began her love of acting and the whole creative process of putting on a show. After moving to Canberra in 2020, Sylvie immediately joined Canberra Youth Theatre and continued her passion by attending workshops and performing in end of semester showcases. Sylvie is thrilled to be working with amazing actors and is looking forward to performing at the Courtyard Studio. Outside of acting, Sylvie enjoys fashion design and singing.

LATSAMY CARRUTHERS | ERIS

Latsamy is an aspiring young actor. This is her second and biggest production ever, both with Canberra Youth Theatre. In the past three years she has grown to love the theatre, everything from the thrill of performing to an audience to bringing a character to life. She finds she is just uncovering a world of creativity. Latsamy is very excited to be part of such an intricate, original play that accurately deals with the horrors of teenhood. She feels very seen.

ZOE HARRIS | FEY

Zoe has always been interested in performing and started acting in shows in 2018. She has previously performed in four musicals, *Cats, Annie, Aladdin,* and *Beauty and the Beast,* as well as drama classes in school, and other workshops and classes. This is her first professional play and she proud of the work this team is creating, and is very excited to work with everyone.

JUNIPER POTTER | AMELIA

Juniper is in their third year of working with Canberra Youth Theatre, taking part in the weekly workshops, and performing as Elle in *Little Girls Alone in the Woods* and in the ensemble of *Dags*. Juniper loves the way acting and writing lets them get lost inside a character and tell new stories. As one of the original collaborators on the creative developments of *The Initiation*, Juniper is incredibly excited to see it come to life on stage.

TARA SAXENA | CHRIS

Tara has been attending Canberra Youth Theatre's workshops since 2020. This is her second production with the company, previously performing as Lucky in *Little Girls Alone in the Woods*. Tara is excited for everyone to be spooked out by this epic teen horror which she has helped workshop over the past year, and has learnt so much from the experience.

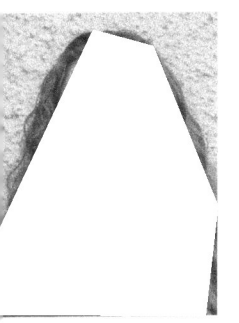

HARRY ZIARNO | LIAM

Harry moved to Canberra in 2020 and started workshops with Canberra Youth Theatre in early 2021. He enjoys the creative collaboration with other artists, especially plot and idea generation. Harry has a keen interest in scriptwriting and pursuing further acting opportunities in any medium. After attending Canberra Youth Theatre productions, Harry is excited to be cast in *The Initiation* as his first production and to work with a team to bring the show to life.

CATHY PETOCZ | PLAYWRIGHT & DIRECTOR

Cathy Petocz is a Canberra-based theatre artist — a playwright, director, performer, and musician — who works on Ngunnawal/Ngambri Country. Cathy's work orbits around a core of pan-Christian mystic spirituality, intersectional feminism, and neurodiversity. She noticed she had been writing protagonists who were all monsters — ghosts, aliens, zombies — each obsessed with trying to understand what it is to be a human, a common experience for neurodivergent people. Once she realised she was writing herself over and over she started to grasp the power of her own neurodivergent thinking and now brings it fully into her artistic practice. Cathy writes plays (*Unbecoming*, Canberra Theatre Centre, 2019), experimental art experiences (*Lit Windows*, You Are Here Festival, 2020), and interactive game-based performance (*We, the People*, Museum of Australian Democracy, 2019). She is currently working on a screenplay adaptation of her surreal mother-daughter drama *Hired Mother* and a puppetry work for young audiences about hope during climate crisis called *Goldilocks and the Three Bears a.k.a. The Apocalypse*.

NYX MATHEWS | SET & COSTUME DESIGNER

Nyx Mathews (born on Wurrundjeri Land, Melbourne; lives and works on Ngunnawal Country, Canberra). Mathews is an early-career artist working across mixed-media sculpture, photography, institutional critique, parafiction and new media. Drawing heavily on the visual language of architecture, Mathews' work explores the physical and cultural structures of the 21st century built environment and its impact on human beings. From the amorphous architectonic atmospheres of a small-scale sculpture to the explicit institutional critique of recent digital works, Mathews' speculative, materially ambiguous practice leverages the beauty of contemporary urban environments to examine the complex structures of power, exclusion, accessibility and alienation which they are designed to enact. Mathews has exhibited work in Melbourne, Canberra and Sydney, including two solo exhibitions and multiple two- and three-person exhibitions. Mathews' work has been curated into group exhibitions locally and interstate. They have received multiple awards and scholarships, including the Drill Hall Gallery Acquisitive Prize (2021), PhotoAccess Residency Award (2021), Peter & Lena Karmel Honours Scholarship in the School of Art (2020), and multiple awards for their third year body of work. Mathews has twice received an ANU Chancellor's Commendation of Outstanding Academic Performance. Their work is held in the permanent collection of Drill Hall Gallery, and in private collections in Australia and overseas.

GILLIAN SCHWAB | LIGHTING DESIGNER

Gillian Schwab is a lighting and production designer for theatre, opera, contemporary music, and circus. In her 18 year career, Gillian has had the privilege of working with a variety of local and national companies including The Street, Big hART, Finucane & Smith, serious, Aspen Island, and Boho Interactive. She has also had the great fortune to create lighting designs for solo works of Australian Performing Arts Legends William Zappa and Graham Bond. Gillian's past designs for Canberra Youth Theatre include *Normal*, *The Worst Band In The Universe*, and the 40 year anniversary season of *Through A Looking Glass*.

PATRICK HAESLER | SOUND DESIGNER

Patrick Haesler is a composer, performer, sound designer and recording artist from Canberra, Australia. Beginning as a trumpeter, Patrick has since branched into numerous musical fields, drawing influences from jazz and progressive music. In 2018 Patrick entered the world of theatre, acting as musical director for ANU's Arts Revue. Since then, he has reprised this role, as well as composing music and designing sound for several theatre productions. These include: *It's Not Creepy If They're Hot*, *Macbeth*, *The Tempest*, *Twelfth Night*, and *Dracula*. In 2021, Patrick's soundtrack for *Macbeth* was released as *The Scottish Album (Original Theatre Soundtrack)*, featuring a host of talented guest musicians and collaborators performing original compositions. Patrick's experience with a wide variety of musical genres, ensembles and production techniques have made him a versatile creative in the world of music and sound.

CAITLIN BAKER | ASSISTANT DIRECTOR

Caitlin Baker is an emerging actor, director, and theatre maker, heading into her fourth year of Arts/Law (Hon) at ANU. In 2022, Caitlin will be taking the helm as President of the ANU Shakespeare Society, producing their largest season yet, Kiss/Kill. This follows her performance in their inaugural production of *Much Ado About Nothing*, and her direction of *The Tempest*. Over the past few years, Caitlin has been deeply involved in the Canberra theatre scene, with other credits including Canberra Repertory Society shows *Grapes of Wrath*, *Brighton Beach Memoirs*, and *The Governor's Family*, and most recently, the inaugural Emerge Company's *Carpe DM*. Deeply invested in the necessity of live performance, Caitlin is thrilled to take the next step in her career with Canberra Youth Theatre, where she is currently a Resident Artist.

RHILEY WINNETT | STAGE MANAGER

Rhiley Winnett has stage managed *Normal*, *Little Girls Alone in the Woods*, *Two Twenty Somethings Decide Never to be Stressed About Anything Ever Again. Ever*, and *Dags* for Canberra Youth Theatre. Rhiley has also stage managed Echo Theatre Company's *Wolf Lullaby*, three shows at college, and works at Erindale Theatre. Rhiley is a dedicated stage manager and is passionate about being part of the new and emerging generation of artists and performers and enjoys watching and learning alongside them as they change and evolve the theatrical industry for the future.

CANBERRA YOUTH THEATRE

STAFF

ARTISTIC DIRECTOR & CEO
LUKE ROGERS

ADMINISTRATOR & WORKSHOPS MANAGER
HELEN WOJTAS

ASSOCIATE PRODUCER
BONNIE CURTIS

FINANCE & STRATEGY MANAGER
LOUISE DAVIDSON

MARKETING & ENGAGEMENT MANAGER
CHRISTOPHER CARROLL

ADMINISTRATION & MARKETING COORDINATOR
THEA JADE

RESIDENT ARTISTS

CAITLIN BAKER
SOPHIE TALLIS

COMMISSIONED WRITERS

JOANNA RICHARDS

BOARD

KAREN VICKERY (CHAIR)
CHRIS WAGNER (DEPUTY CHAIR)
PETER HOOLIHAN (SECRETARY)
TESSA HAMMOND (TREASURER)
ELLEN HARVEY
CASSANDRA HOOLIHAN
ADRIANA LAW
CELIA RIDEAUX

WORKSHOP ARTISTS

CHRISTOPHER CARROLL
ELLIOT CLEAVES
ANNA JOHNSTONE
HOLLY JOHNSON
TOBI ODUSOTE
CHARLOTTE PALMER
CATHY PETOCZ
JENA PRINCE
RACHEL ROBERTSON
YLARIA ROGERS

GORMAN ARTS CENTRE
H BLOCK - BATMAN STREET BRADDON ACT 2612

02 6248 5057
INFO@CANBERRAYOUTHTHEATRE.COM.AU

CANBERRAYOUTHTHEATRE.COM.AU

  @canberrayouththeatre

50 YEARS YOUNG

From our early beginnings as Canberra Children's Theatre, through the Youth Theatre Workshop years of the 1970s, and decades more as Canberra Youth Theatre, we are now one of the leading youth arts companies in Australia.

In 1981, Canberra Youth Theatre moved from its first home at Reid House to Gorman Arts Centre where we are still a resident company, and have since collaborated with thousands of young artists through productions, workshops, creative developments and community events.

As an ACT Key Arts Organisation, we have created work across all of Canberra: in our major theatres, public spaces, and national cultural institutions. We have toured around the country, and internationally.

Canberra Youth Theatre has grown and evolved significantly over the past five decades, constantly responding to the passions and perspectives of generations of young people, and adapting to changes in the way we create and experience live performance. We remain at the forefront of Australian youth theatre practice, creating innovative, accessible and challenging opportunities for young people to access and engage in professional-quality theatrical experiences.

Through decades of turmoil and many triumphs, our wonderful company has continued to nurture and develop young people, giving them a place to belong, to share their voice, and to inspire audiences of all ages. It is an amazing legacy to celebrate.

Here we are, the voice of youth expressed through challenging and intelligent theatre. 50 years young, and loving every minute of it!

OUR PARTNERS

Ainslie and Gorman Arts Centres

THE JEREMY SPENCER BROOM LEGACY

ELECT PRINTING

www.ingramcontent.com/pod-product-compliance
Lightning Source LLC
Chambersburg PA
CBHW050023090426
42734CB00021B/3399